For my true love, my children, family and friends who've been integral in my manifestation journey.

978-1-7367142-0-1
Imprint: Nsprirational Art Publishing

You have the ability to create any life you want for yourself. You want more money, it's yours. New house, new job, better relationship, or any relationship for that matter; all of these things can be yours just by the renewing of your thoughts.

The purpose of this daily journal, is to help you focus your thoughts and energy into one space, and through that practice, create the world in which you want to live in.
As you go through each page, you will plant the seeds, or write the feelings you want to experience in the lower half of the circle. Then in the top half of the circle describe the corresponding fruit, or the visual representation to the feelings you have planted.

In addition to "planting" your seeds, you will have three lines beneath the diagram where you can describe three positive things you want to manifest in your life today. That could be just as simple as saying I am so happy that my best friend and I are meeting for brunch. Or I'm so grateful now that my boss has offered me more money at work.
As time goes on you will begin to see the world around you change. Practice this daily and you will be amazed at what you bring into existence.

Finally, on the back of each page describe in as much detail the things you want in your life today. A new pair of shoes, a partner, a new dishwasher... Sky's the limit. It is only your job to say what you want, and focus on the clear picture of what those things are.

I wish you love, light, and immense peace and blessings as you embark on your New Life Creation.


- A. Brenee

**Date: 01/01/01**

Fruit

Purchased a new home,
married, children, traveling,
new job, great friends, financial
independence

---

Abundance, Love, Home,

Relationships, commitment,

dedication

Seeds

1. Today I'm so happy and grateful now that I am in the process of buying my first home.

"I am so happy and grateful now that I am growing my family. I've desired to have more children, and now my dreams are coming to pass. I am so happy that my husband and I are welcoming our new baby boy into this world in a family full of love and appreciation. Things may not always be easy, but the lessons I'm learning along this journey are valued and appreciated"

# Who Am I....

Only using positive words, describe the version of yourself that you want to be... in the present tense!

Now that you know who you are, you can begin your journey into living the version of life, that the New You lives... Enjoy the process.

**Date:**

Fruit

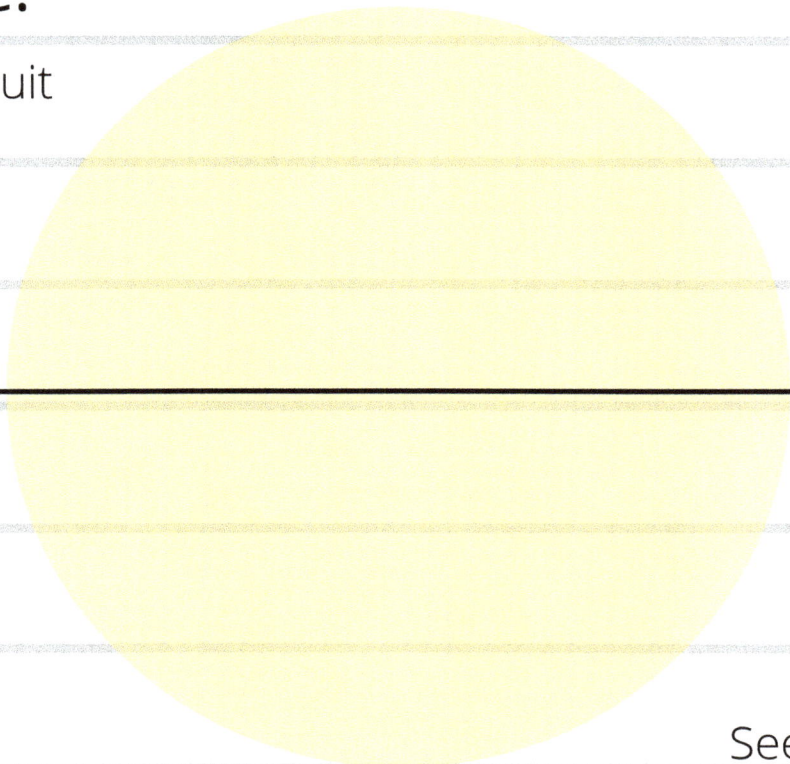

Seeds

1.

2.

3.

**Date:**

Fruit

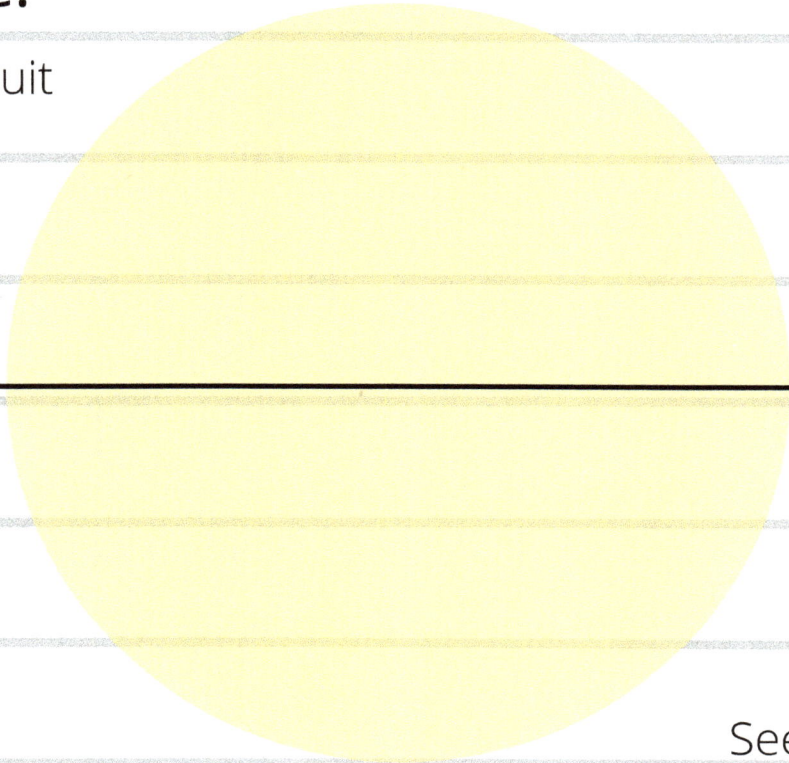

_____

Seeds

1.

2.

3.

**Date:**

Fruit

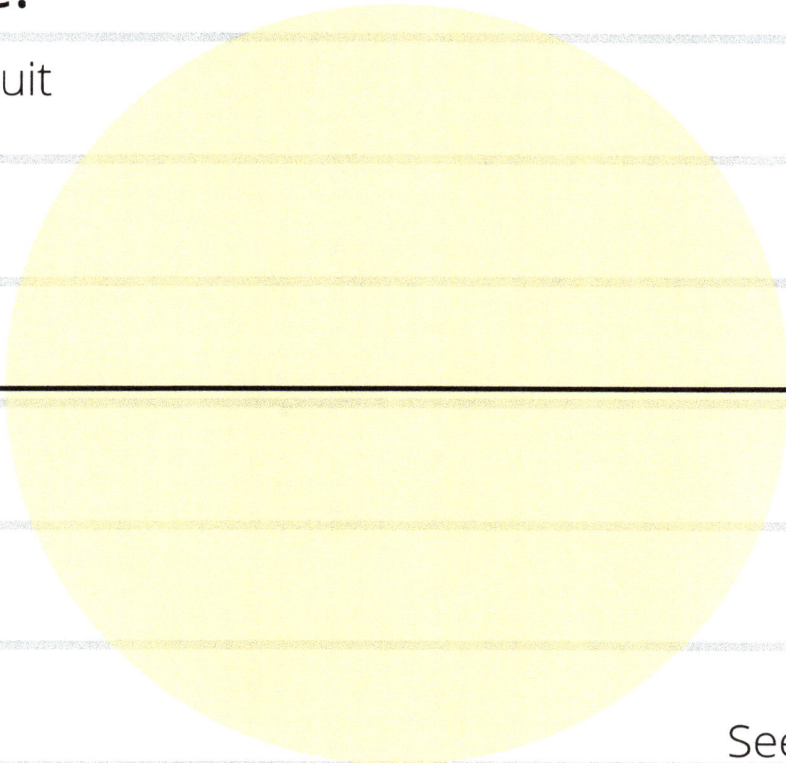

Seeds

1.

2.

3.

# Date:

Fruit

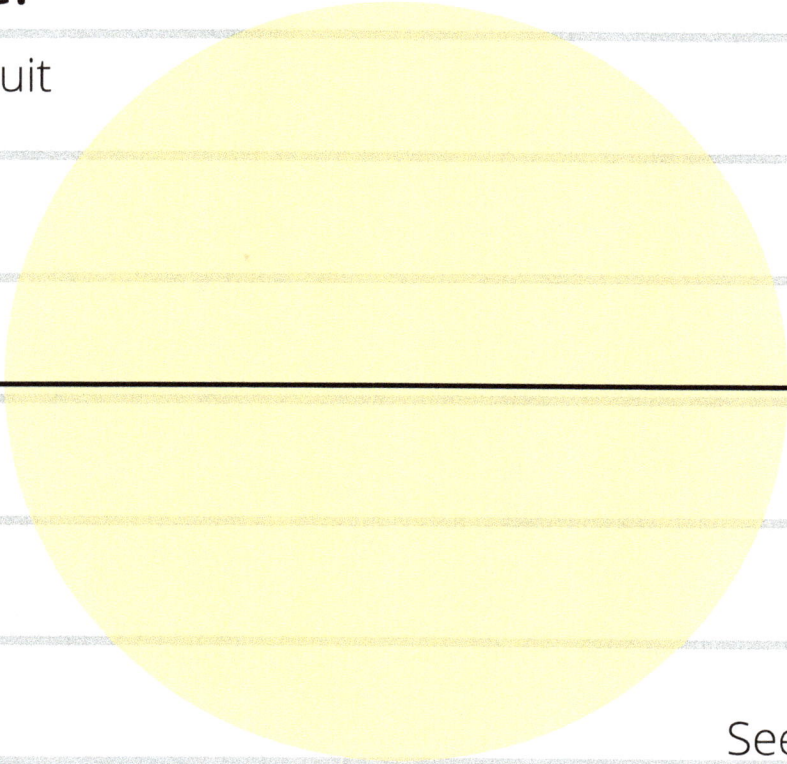

Seeds

1.

2.

3.

**Date:**

Fruit

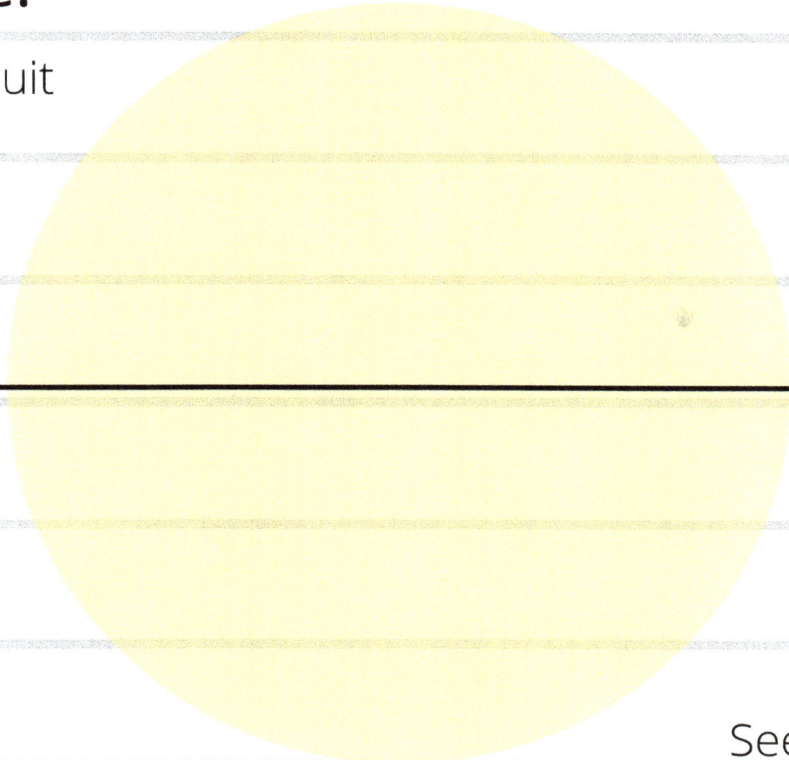

Seeds

1.

2.

3.

**Date:**

Fruit

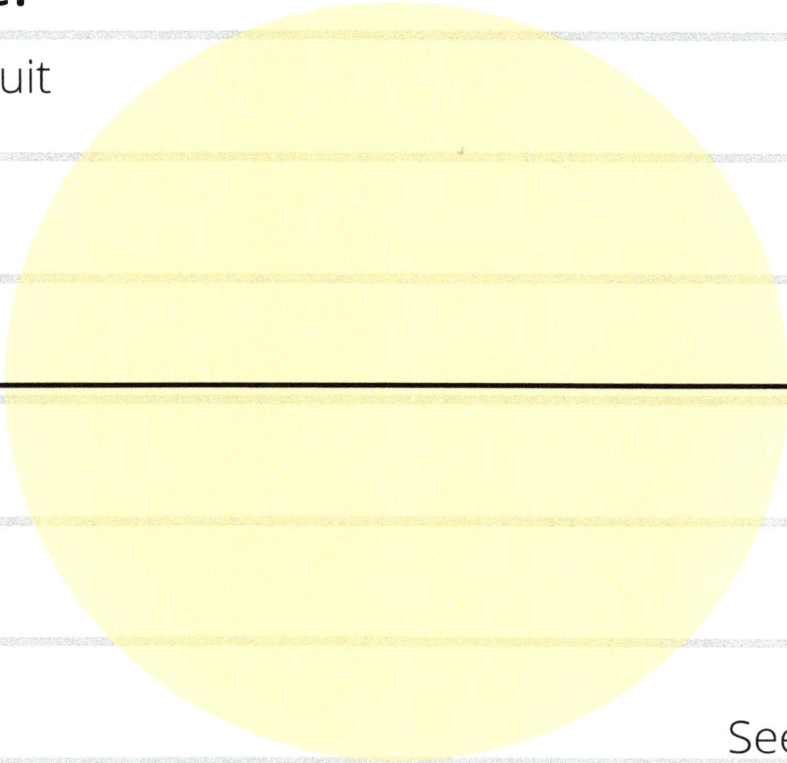

Seeds

1.

2.

3.

**Date:**

Fruit

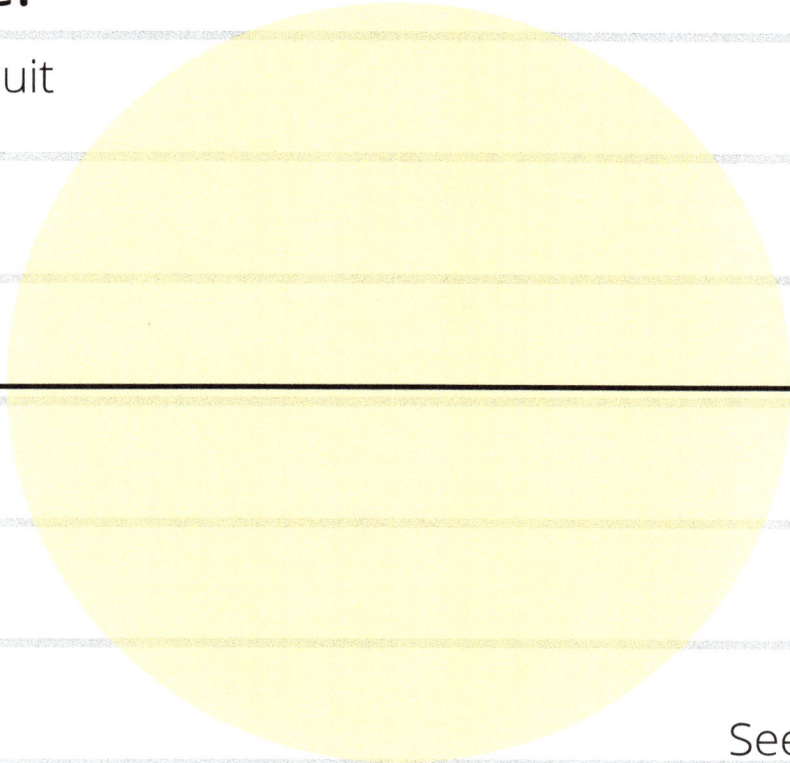

Seeds

1.

2.

3.

**Date:**

Fruit

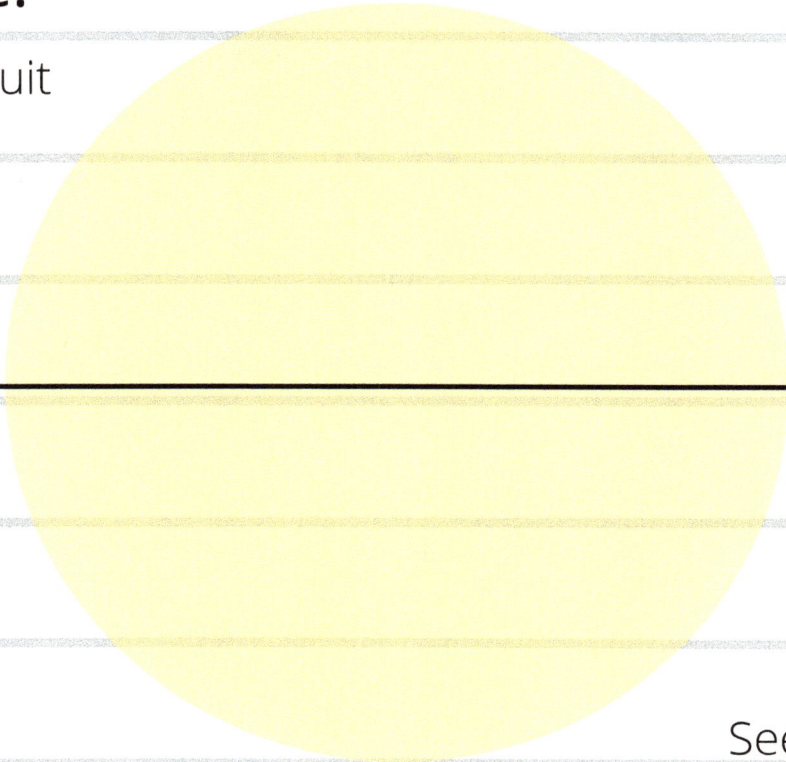

Seeds

1.

2.

3.

## Date:

Fruit

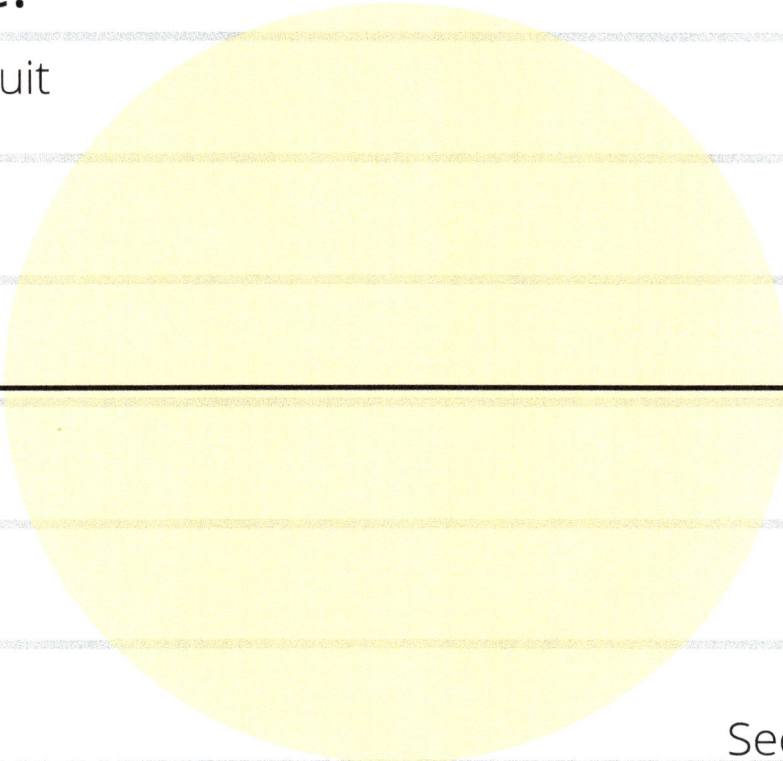

Seeds

1.

2.

3.

**Date:**

Fruit

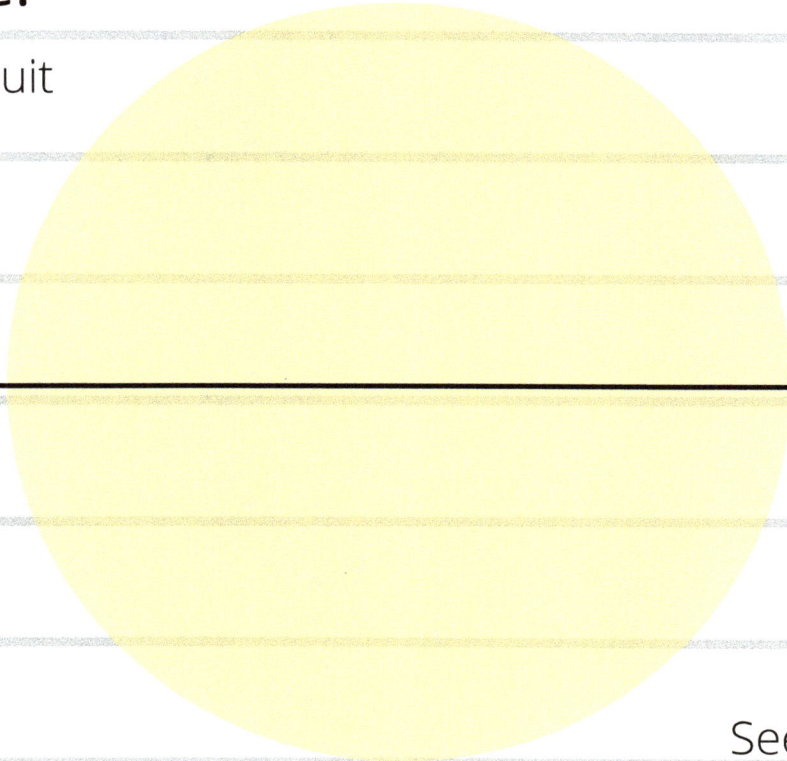

Seeds

1.

2.

3.

**Date:**

Fruit

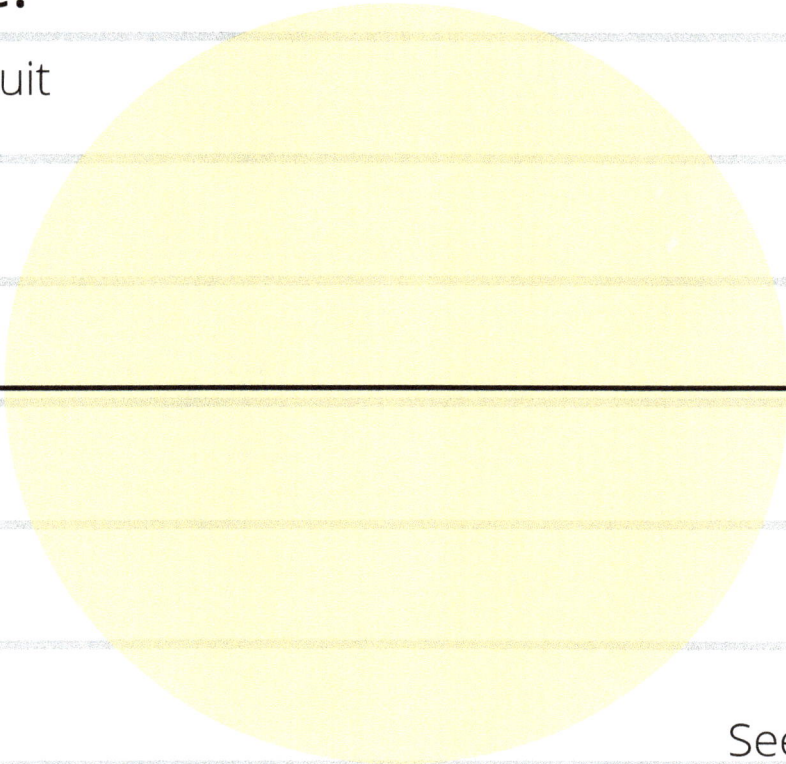

Seeds

1.

2.

3.

**Date:**

Fruit

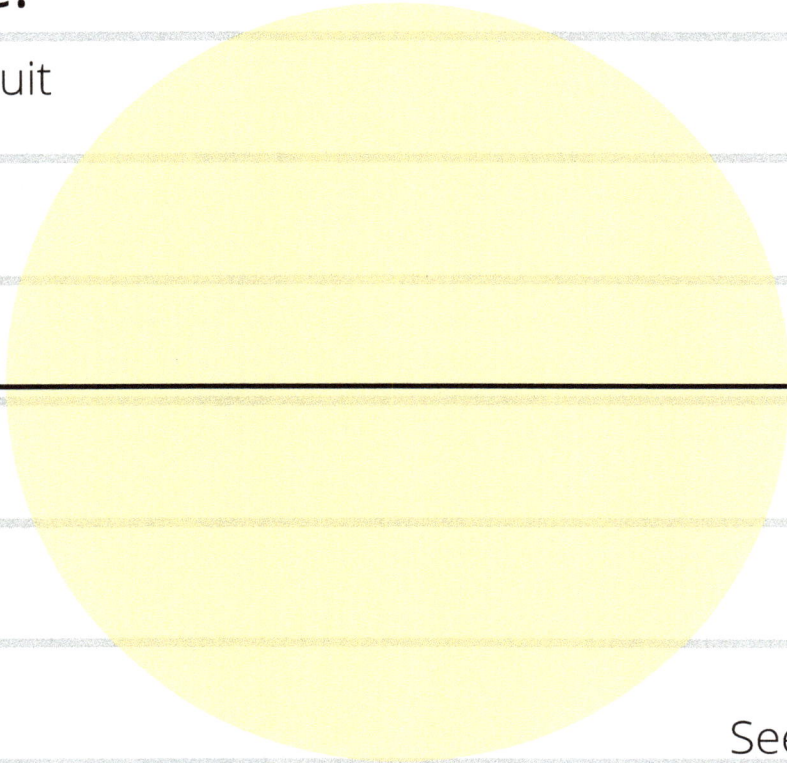

Seeds

1.

2.

3.

**Date:**

Fruit

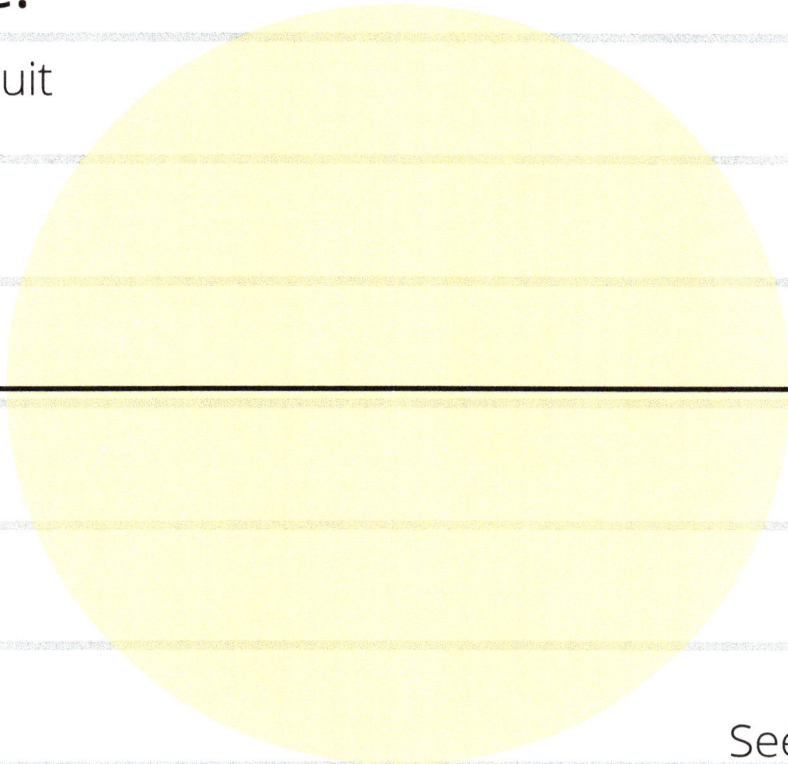

Seeds

1.

2.

3.

# Date:

Fruit

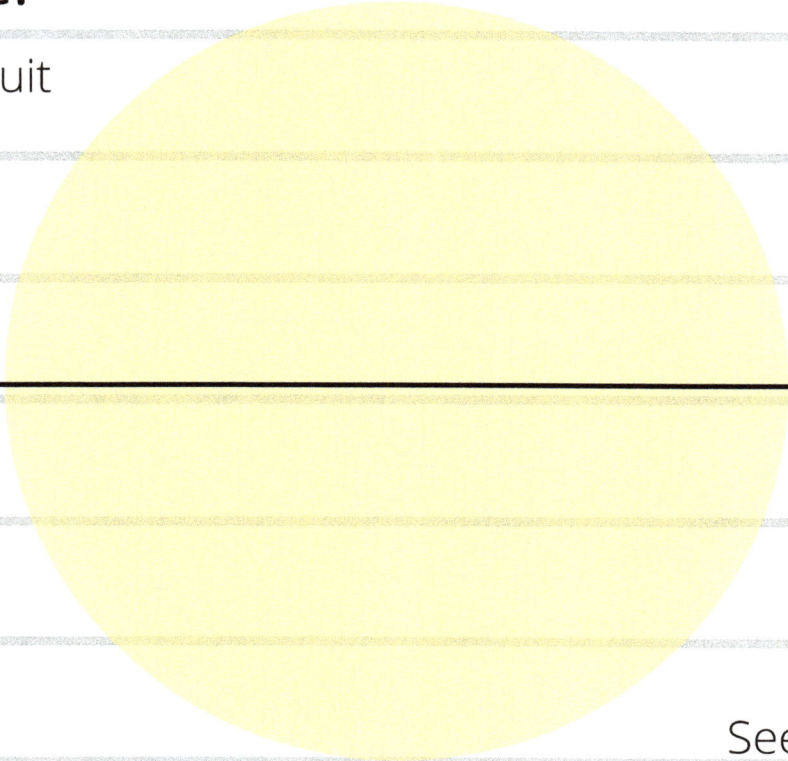

Seeds

1.

2.

3.

**Date:**

Fruit

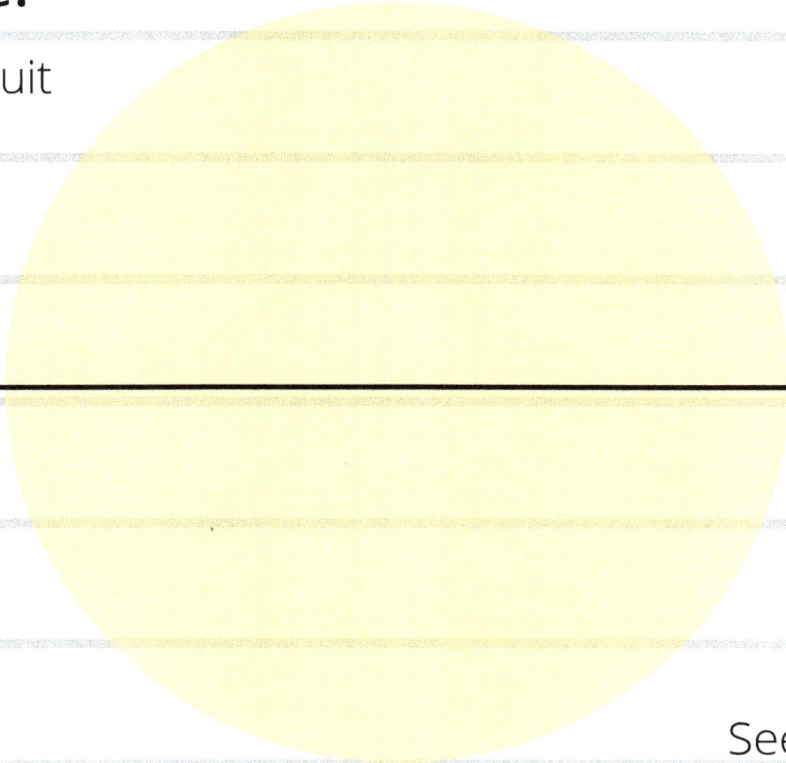

Seeds

1.

2.

3.

**Date:**

Fruit

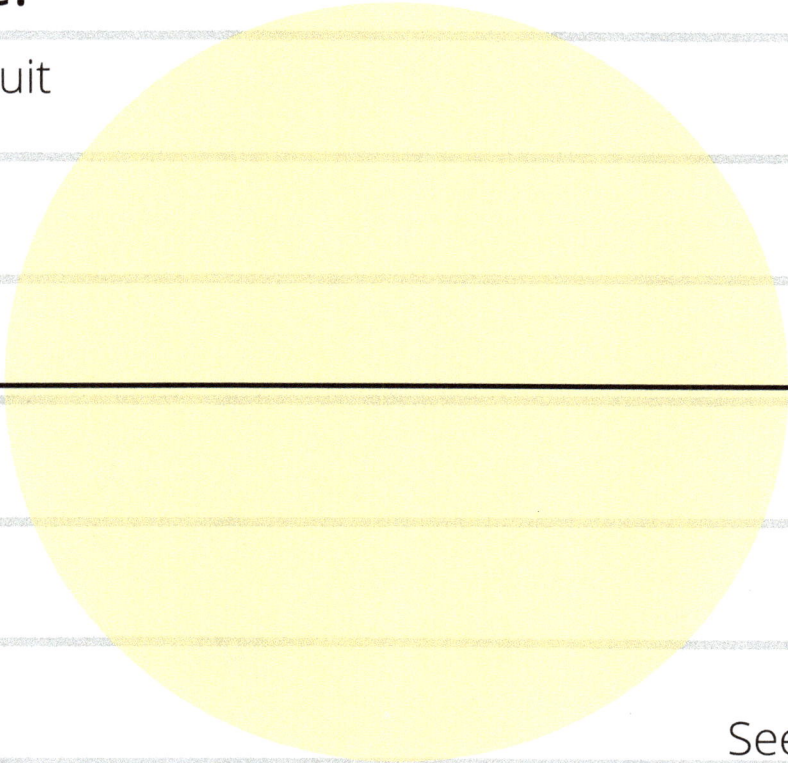

Seeds

1.

2.

3.

**Date:**

Fruit

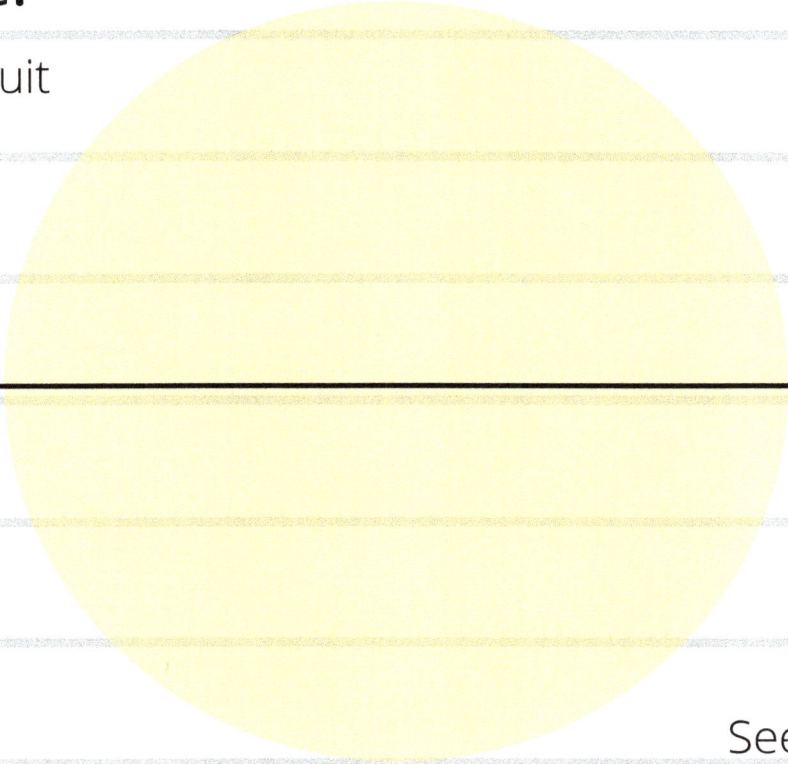

Seeds

1.

2.

3.

**Date:**

Fruit

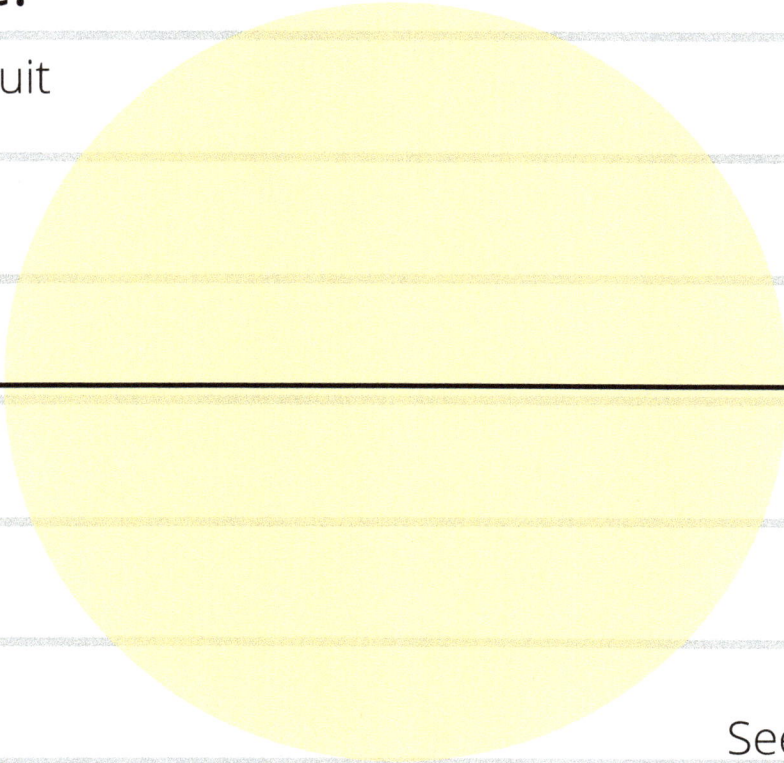

Seeds

1.

2.

3.

**Date:**

Fruit

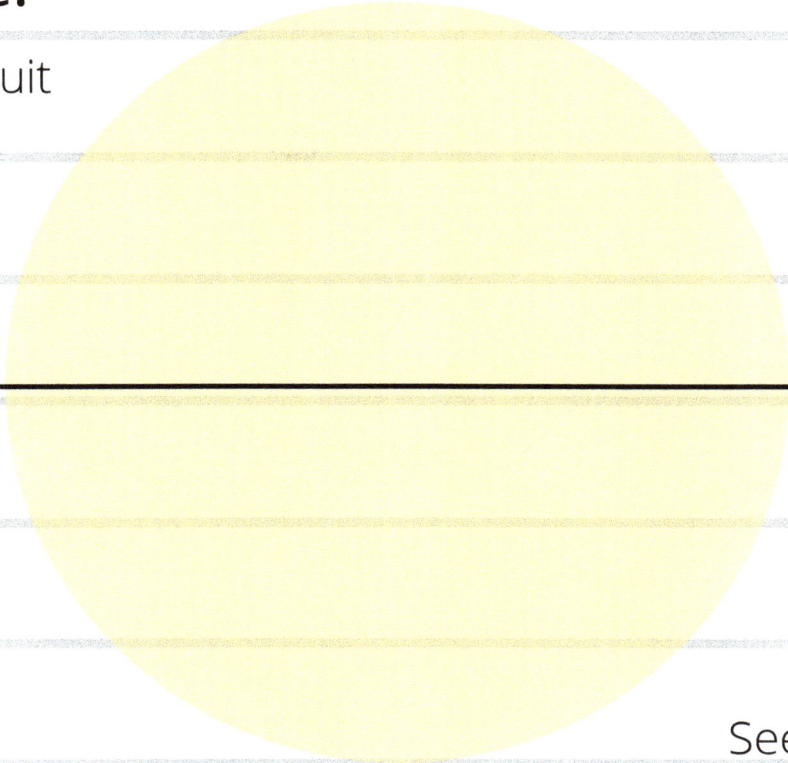

Seeds

1.

2.

3.

**Date:**

Fruit

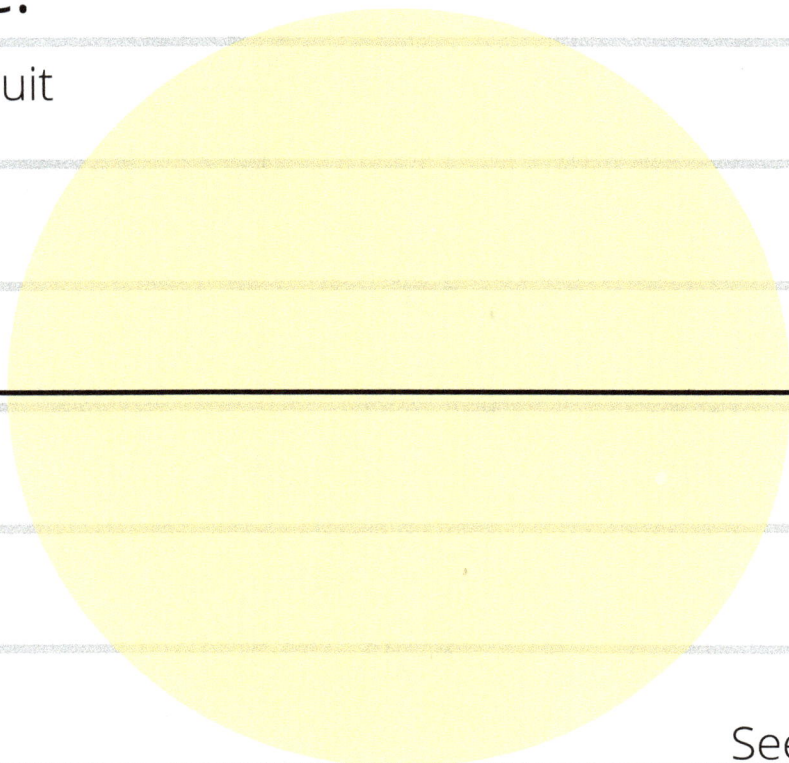

_____

Seeds

1.

2.

3.

**Date:**

Fruit

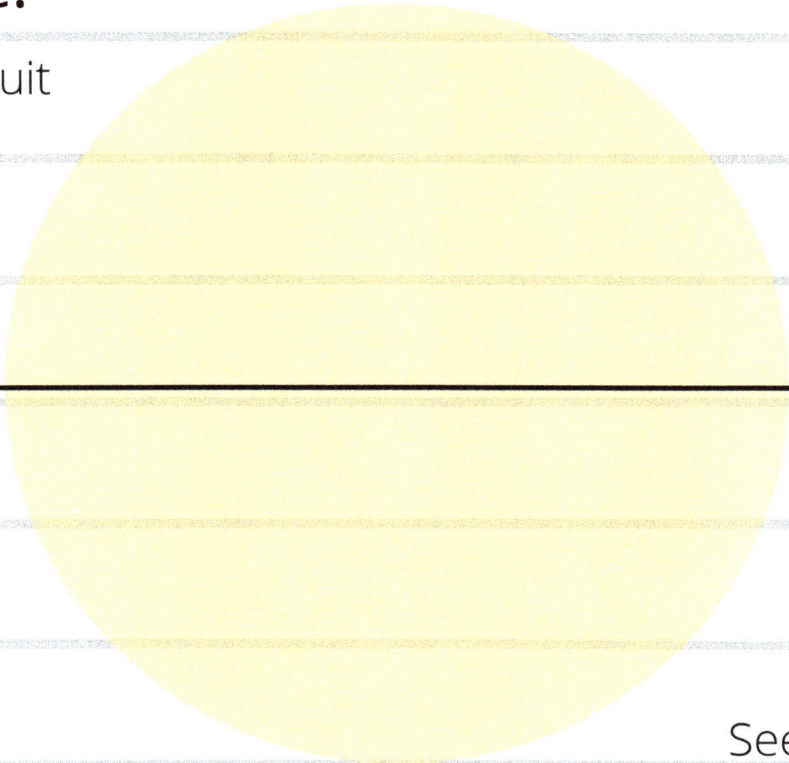

Seeds

1.

2.

3.

**Date:**

Fruit

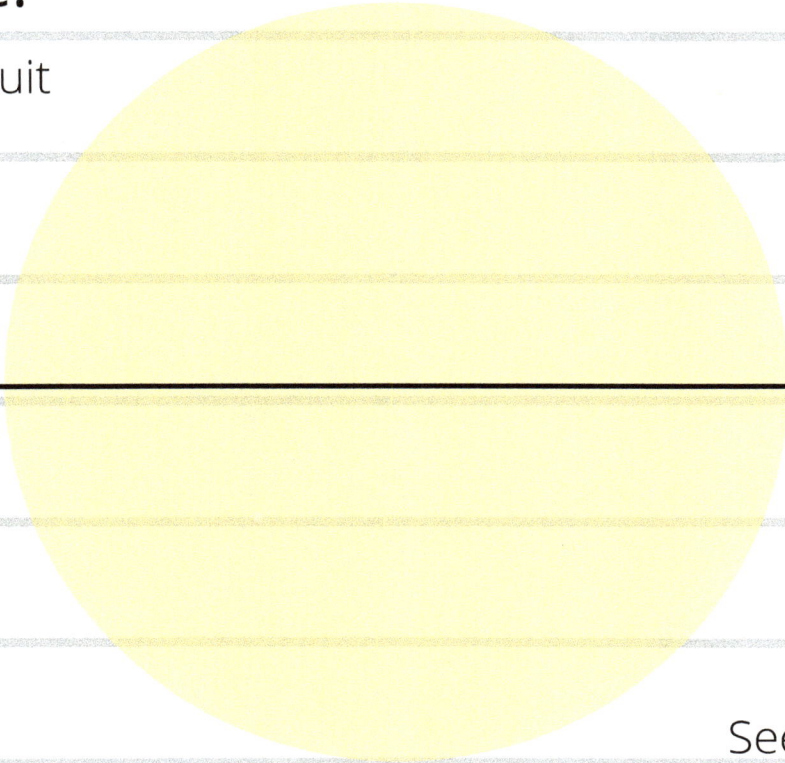

_____

Seeds

1.

2.

3.

**Date:**

Fruit

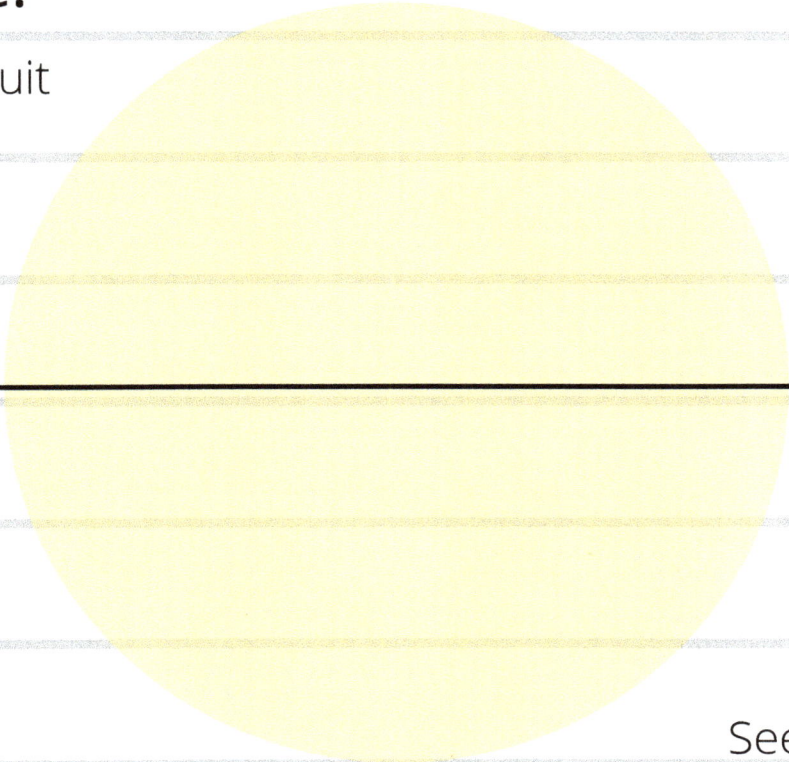

_____

Seeds

1.

2.

3.

**Date:**

Fruit

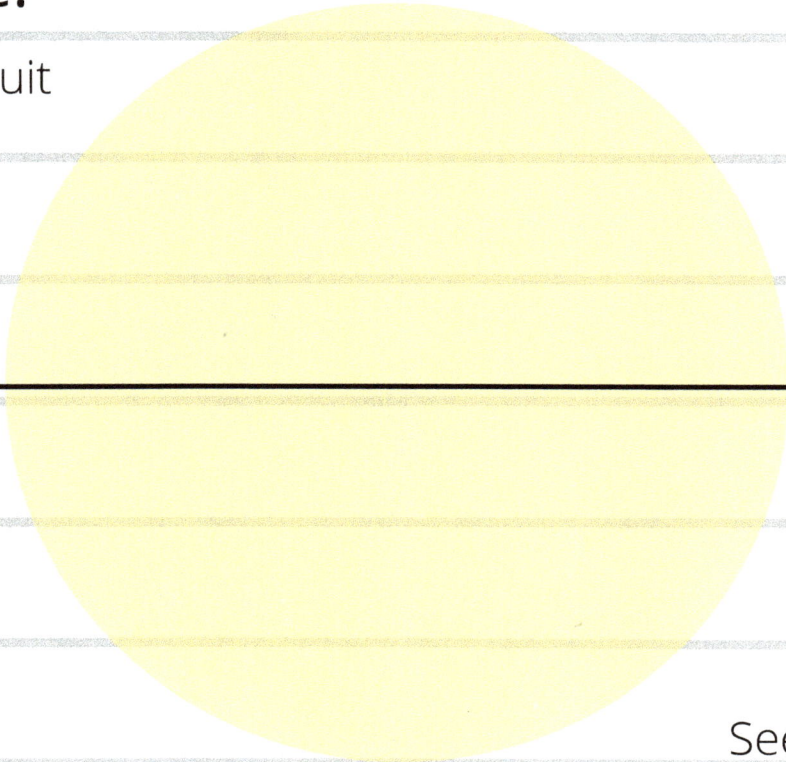

_____

Seeds

1.

2.

3.

**Date:**

Fruit

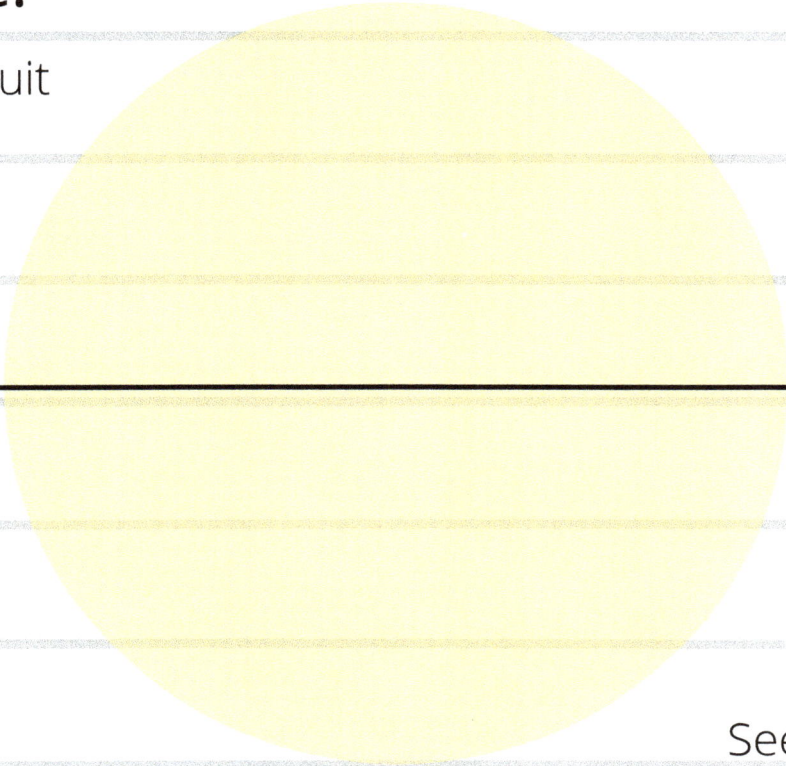

_____

Seeds

1.

2.

3.

# Date:

Fruit

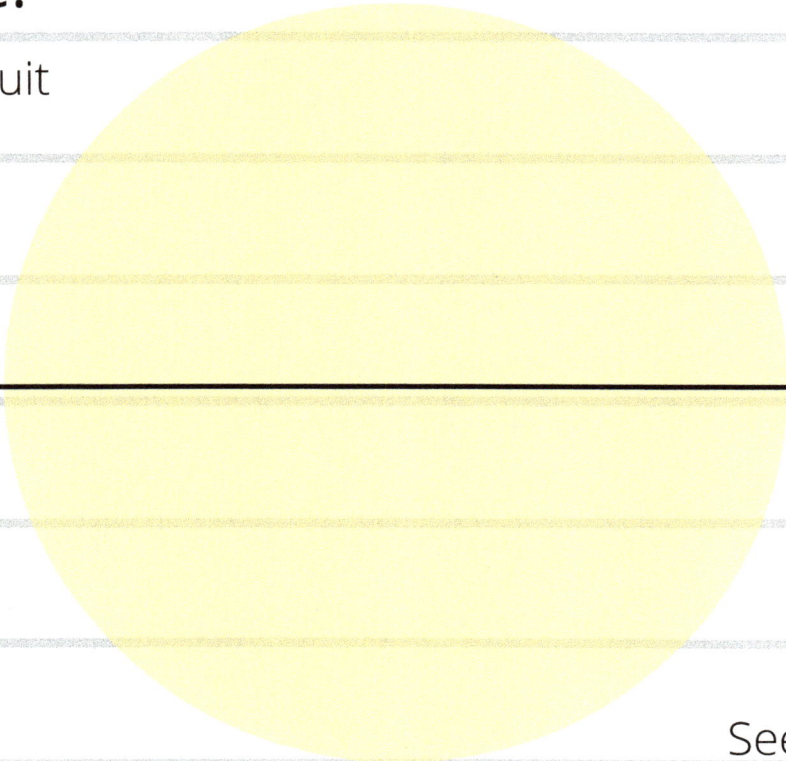

Seeds

1.

2.

3.

**Date:**

Fruit

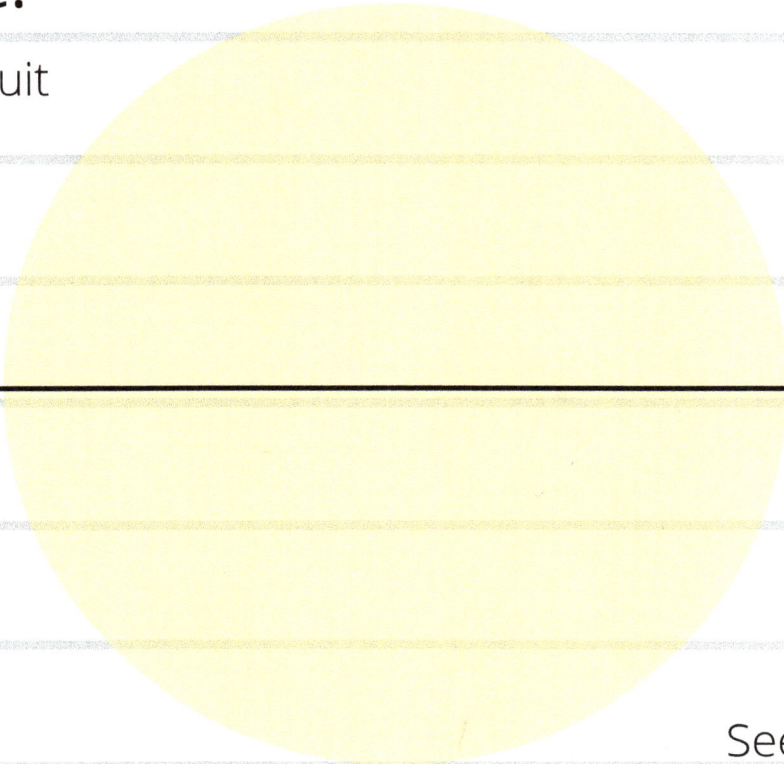

Seeds

1.

2.

3.

**Date:**

Fruit

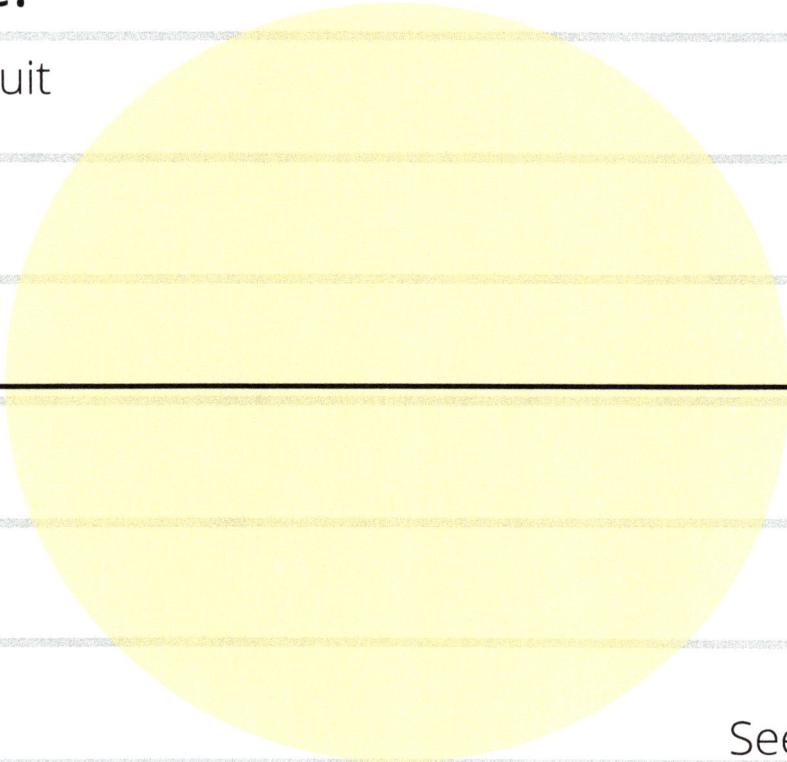

_____

Seeds

1.

2.

3.

**Date:**

Fruit

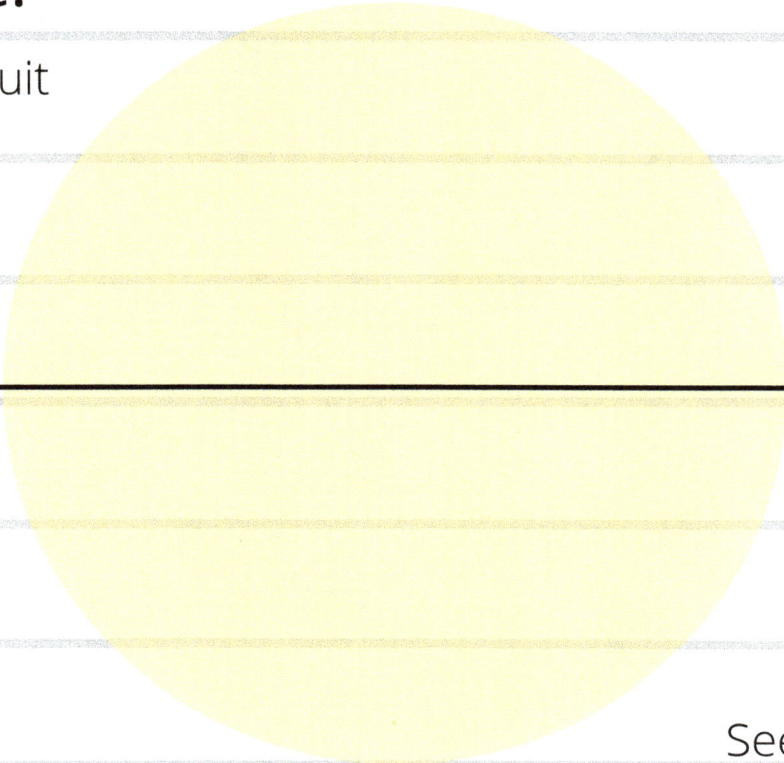

Seeds

1.

2.

3.

**Date:**

Fruit

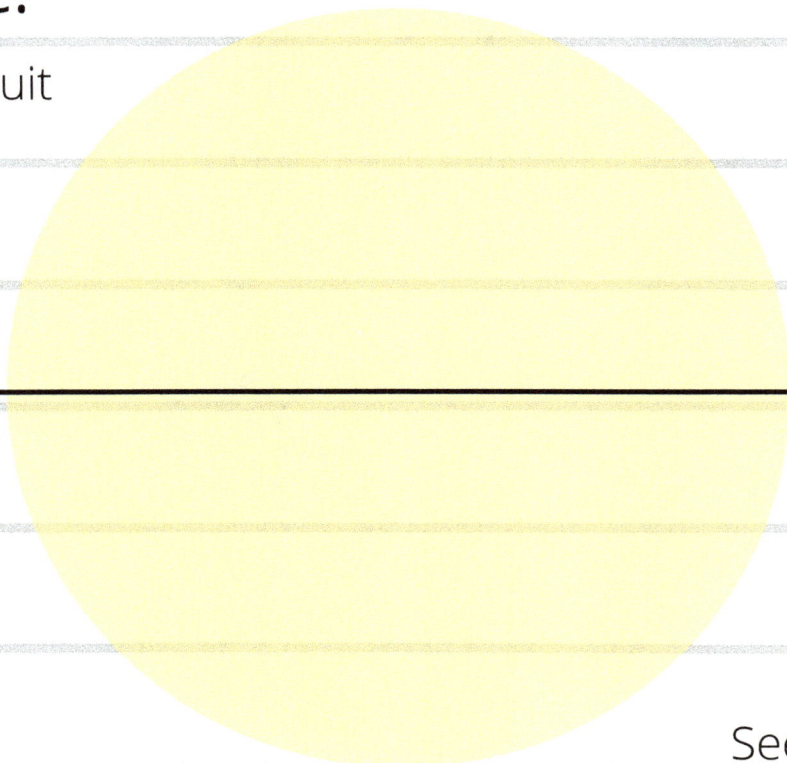

_____

Seeds

1.

2.

3.

**Date:**

Fruit

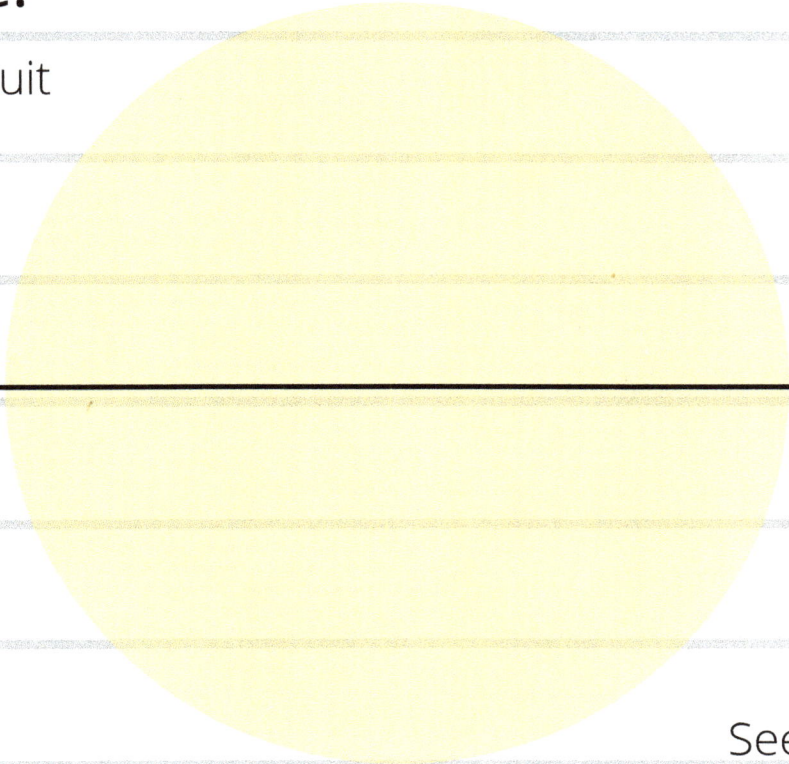

Seeds

1.

2.

3.

**Date:**

Fruit

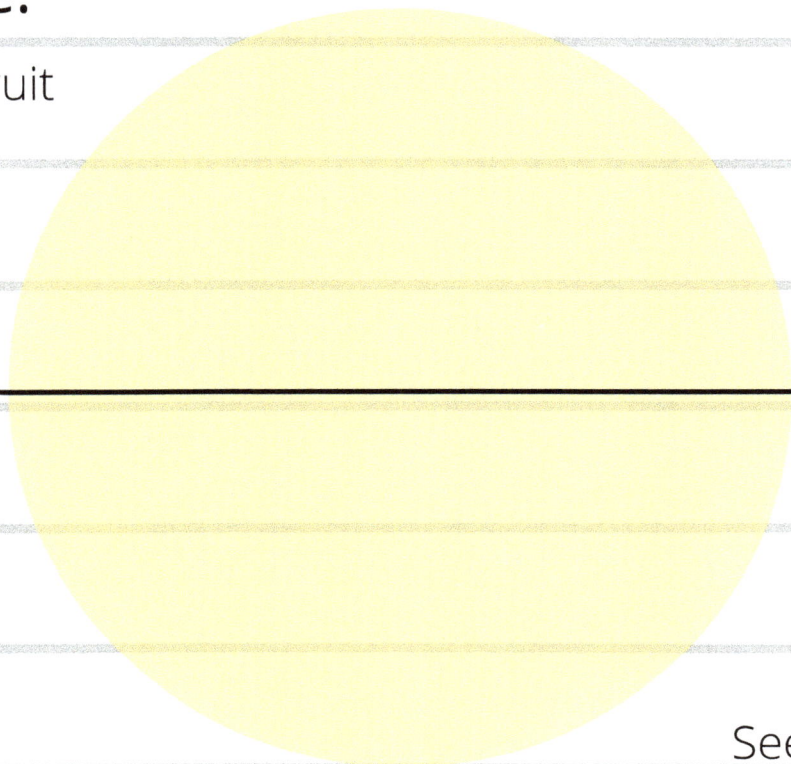

Seeds

1.

2.

3.

**Date:**

Fruit

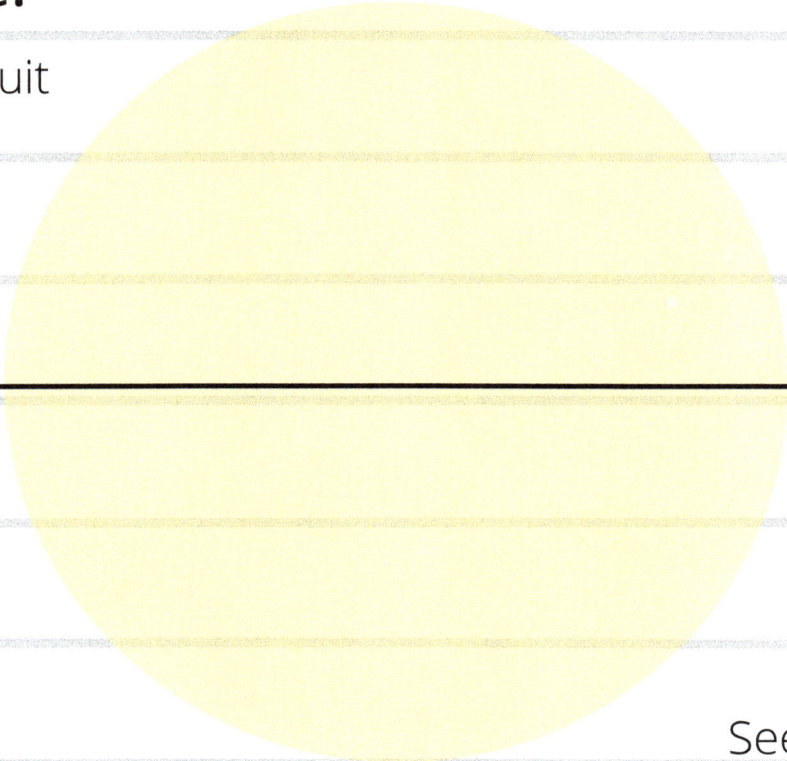

Seeds

1.

2.

3.

**Date:**

Fruit

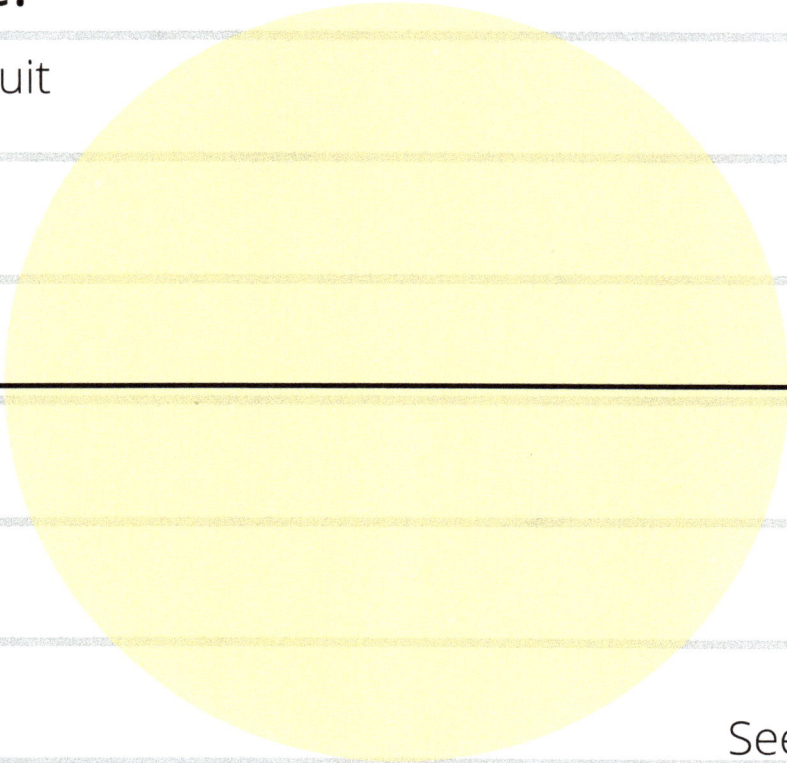

Seeds

1.

2.

3.

**Date:**

Fruit

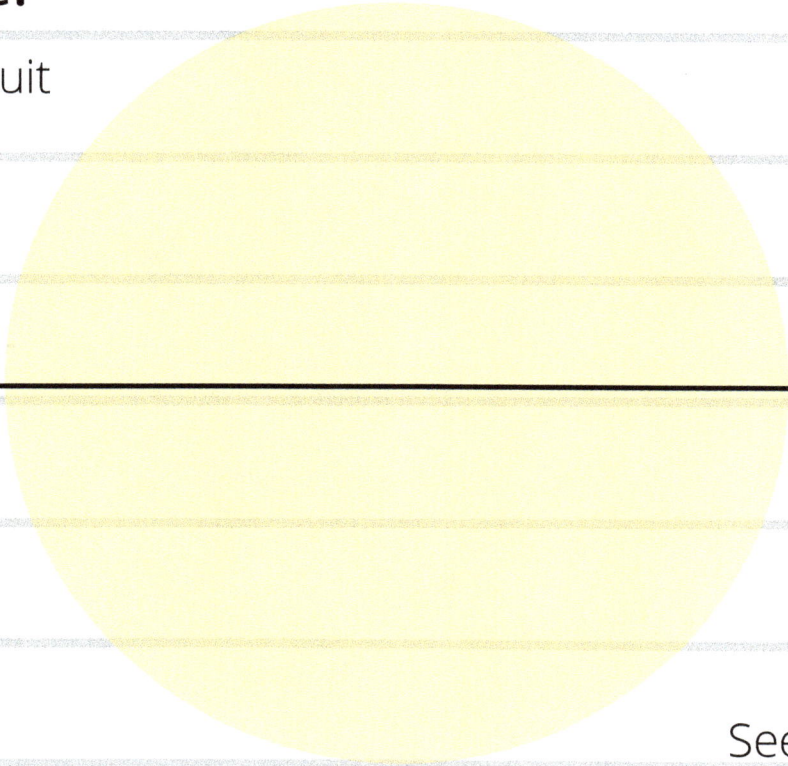

Seeds

1.

2.

3.

**Date:**

Fruit

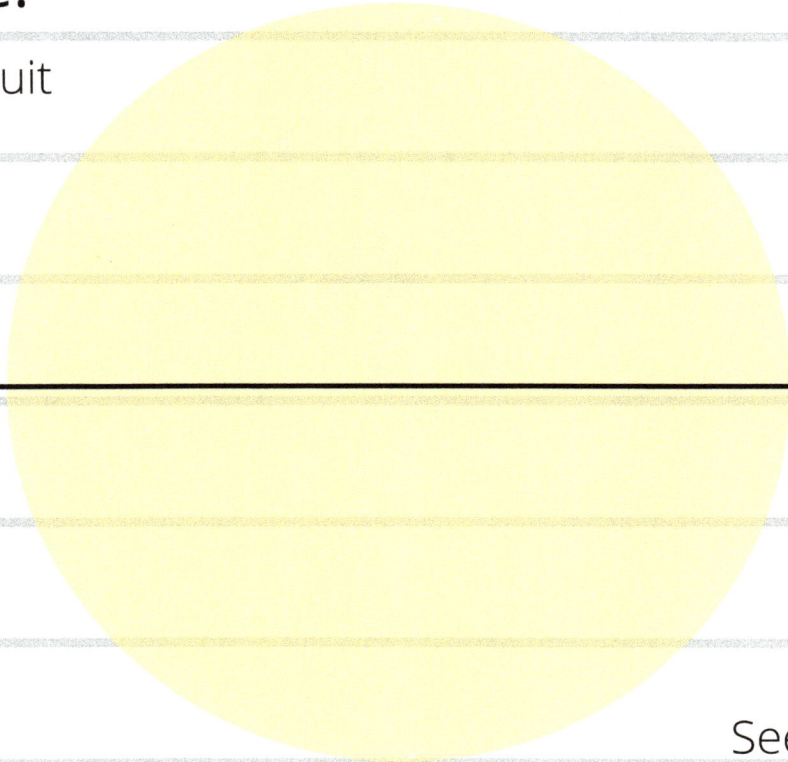

_____

Seeds

1.

2.

3.

**Date:**

Fruit

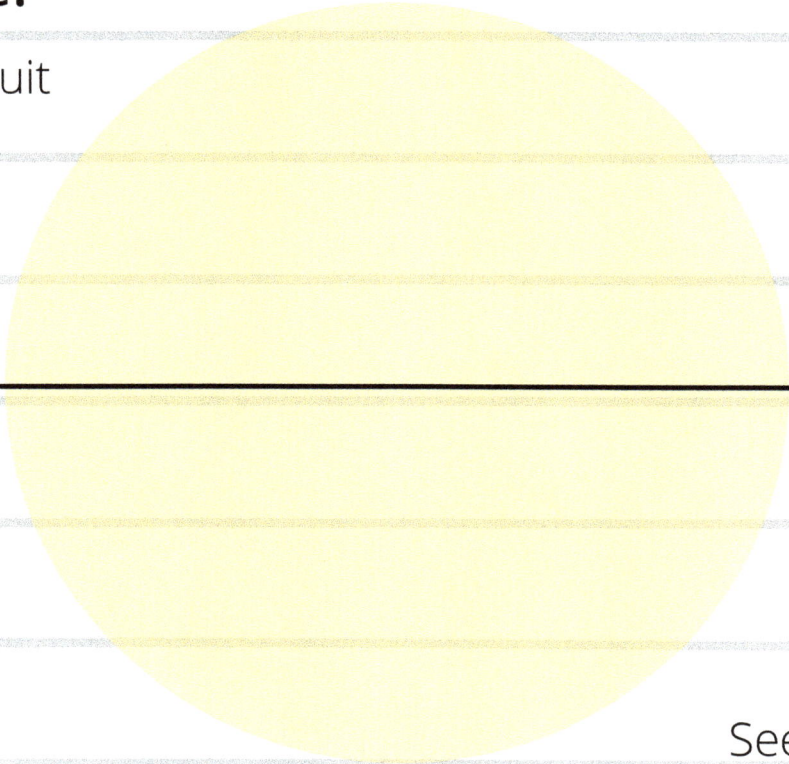

Seeds

1.

2.

3.

**Date:**

Fruit

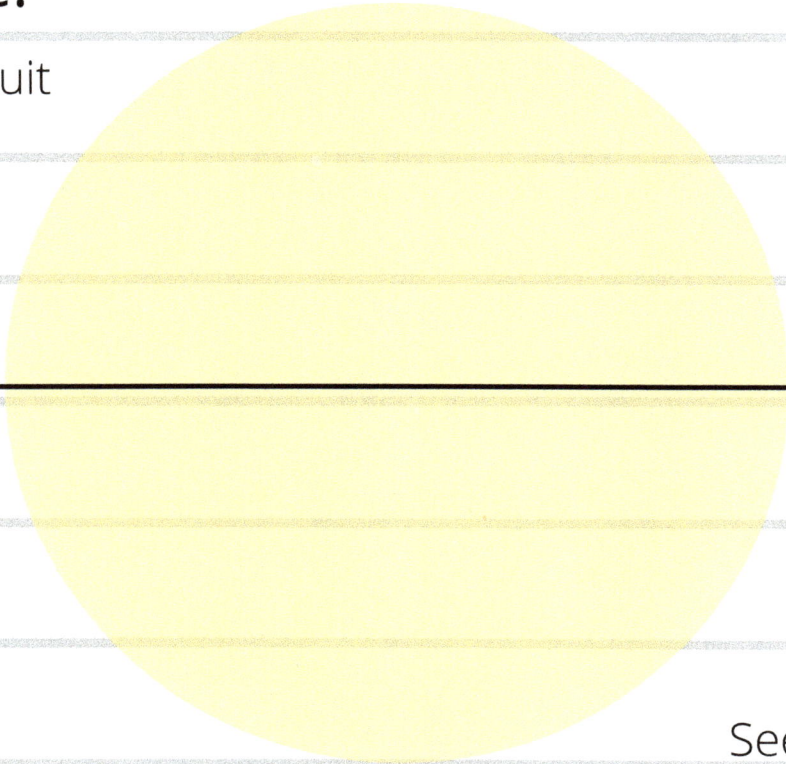

Seeds

1.

2.

3.

**Date:**

Fruit

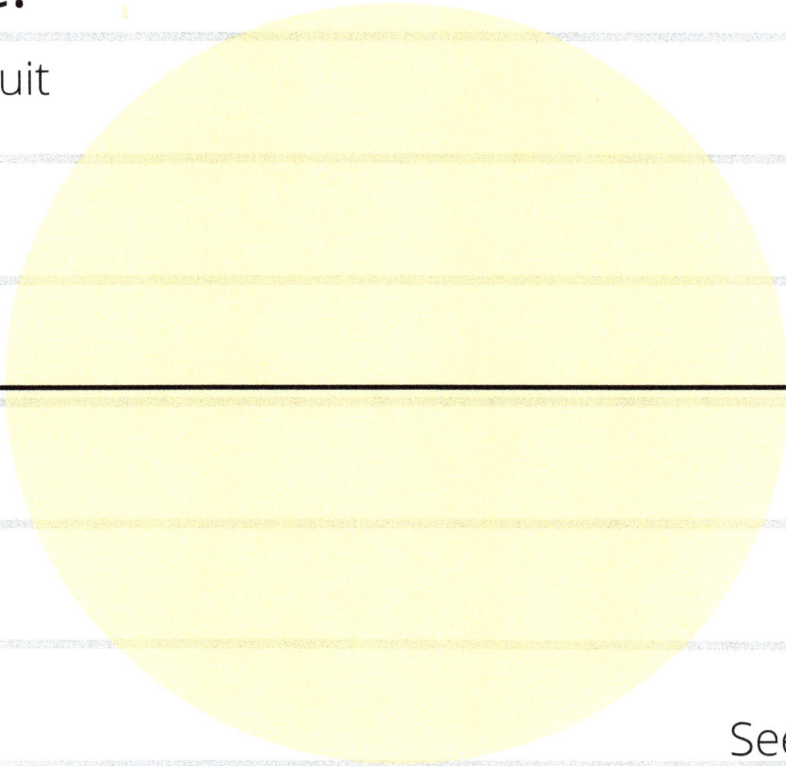

Seeds

1.

2.

3.

**Date:**

Fruit

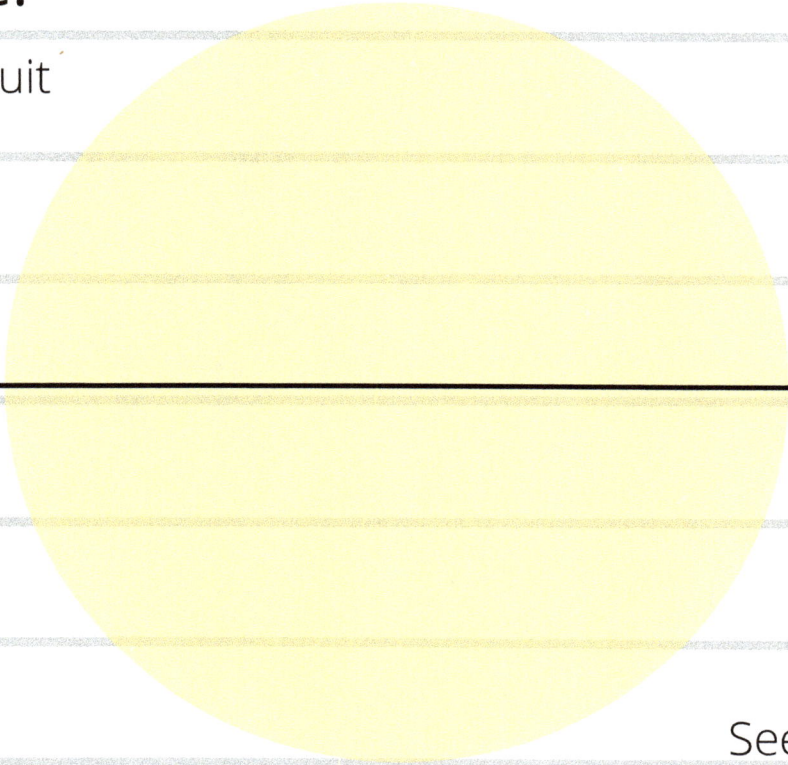

_____

Seeds

1.

2.

3.

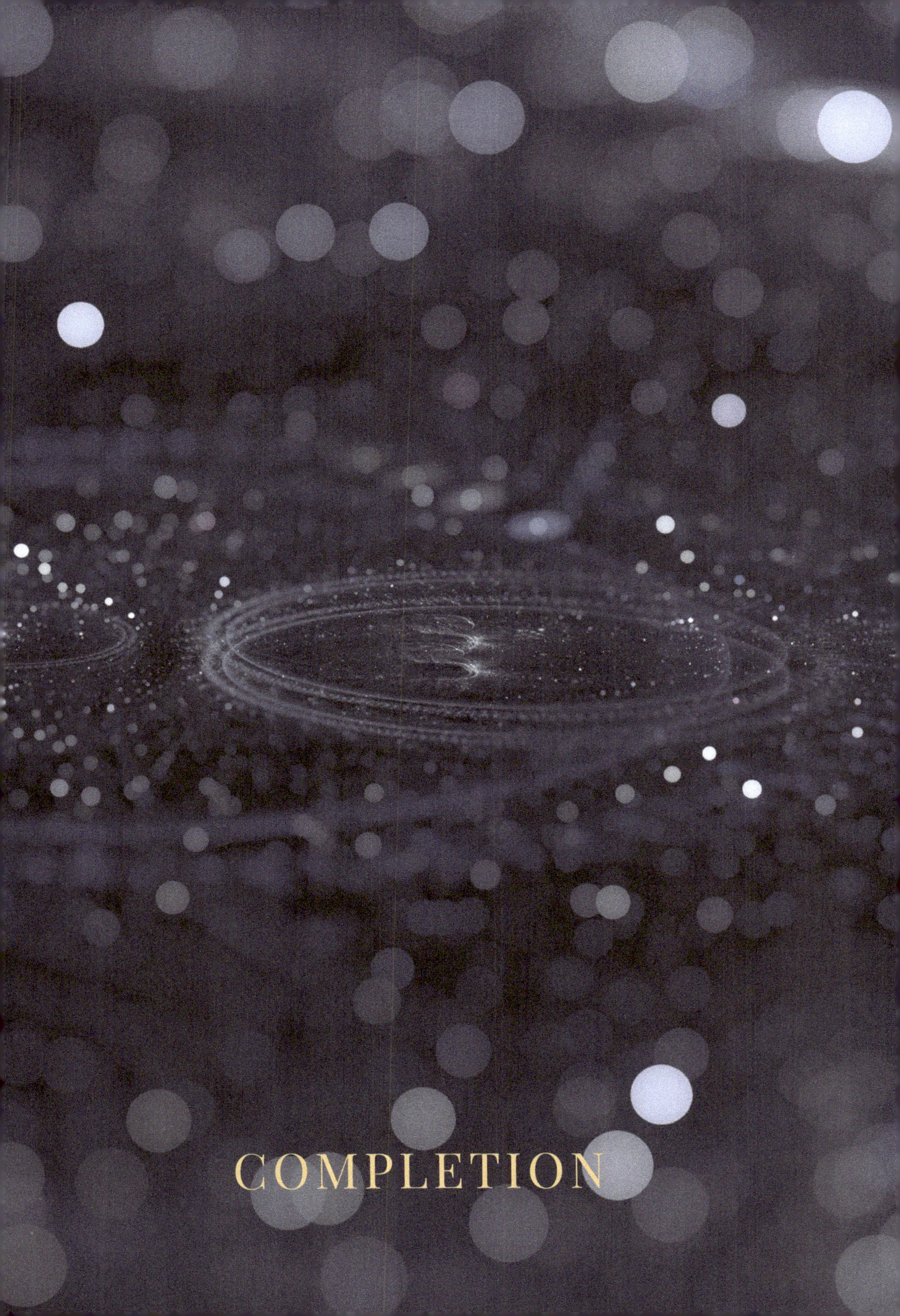

# COMPLETION